Keto Uncooked

Keto Uncooked

Dirty Keto Cheat Codes

Lekisha Williams-Sutton

Lekisha Williams-Sutton

CONTENTS

About the Author

I, Lekisha Williams-Sutton, was born and raised on the Southside of Chicago, IL; but now reside in Powder Springs, GA. I hold both, Undergraduate and Graduate Degrees in Family and Individual Development and Psychology. I am also the Co-Founder of Coffee Snobs: Buy the Cup (a unique and phenomenal upcoming Coffee Shop and experience); and other entrepreneurial endeavors. I have a happy blended family of five.

Definitely no stranger to weight fluctuations and obesity. Hence, my avid research and firsthand experience with the Keto Lifestyle. I act as a catalyst to simplify the Keto Lifestyle in order for it to be less intimidating and easier to embrace for those who may really desire the transition into a lifestyle that helps them to look and feel their best. Making an informed decision, being intrinsically motivated, and confident in the decision to adopt the Keto Lifestyle are my goals for the content of "Keto Uncooked: Dirty Keto Cheat Codes." Please enjoy this guide; and I truly appreciate you for your support!

Introduction

On June 14, 2018; I was rear ended and my vehicle totaled. This accident was pivotal in my decision to change my way of life in regards to food! I sustained several injuries to my spine, underwent several chiropractic sessions, and painful procedures to my spine in an attempt to regain my ability to walk upright unaided. Although the ability was restored after about 6 months; the pain remains, and is intensified when my back is strained in any way. I thought I could accept my new limited mobility and move on.

It was when my then 3yr. old was almost drowned in the tub because my back went out causing me to fall on him while trying to bathe him. Not even natural adrenaline could force me to be able to pull myself up in spite of how much I cried and attempted to will myself to do so. Eventually, my baby slid from under me enabling me to muster up the strength to drag myself out of there. As my baby cried; I decided I had no choice but to accept that I had to subject myself to yet another painful spinal procedure. My Dr. suggested that a fair amount of weight loss would assist greatly in my recovery; and possibly remove my need to continue the spinal procedures that only gave minimal results.

Working out was virtually impossible in my condition. So, I knew it had to be diet alone (at least until I regained enough strength to do it lightly). That is when I discovered Keto! I researched it for several weeks, was honest with myself about my triggers (sweets), located substitutes for them, and jumped in with both feet!

218lbs. was my starting weight. I was down 56lbs. (162lbs.) within 9 months just from doing strict Keto for 1 month (no sweets or bread substitutes), and dirty Keto for the rest of that time frame. I remain at that weight; and never go beyond 170lbs. with newly introduced light cardio and transitioning to low carb/dirty Keto to maintain my progress (I look better not being completely skinny).

Keto has literally saved my quality of life, improved my health and appearance in ways I could never have imagined. I am simply here to share what I did in hopes that it will help others reach their personal goals! I am not a Dr. nor a Keto Specialist, and not at all guaranteeing success for what has simply worked for me and a few close friends who joined me on my journey.

Some of the information may seem complicated initially. Trust that it is easier than it seems once you get your tools, food, and motivation in place to actually do it! Please soak up as much knowledge as possible from what I am sharing, apply it only when you are truly ready to make this life change, NEVER beat yourself up if you relapse occasionally, just remain motivated, take each day as it comes, get back on track, and enjoy your new Keto Lifestyle!

What is Keto; and How Do I Get Started?

In Keto, - low carb, no sugar way of eating - the short version is.... Stay away from sugar, bread, rice, potatoes, yams, vegetable oil, honey and starchy vegetables. The majority of us "Ketoers" do not consume more than 20 carbs and 1200 calories/day. The Carb Manager App is great for customizing your Macros to your specific status and goals. Please start there!

Eat a lot of fat like: butter, hard cheeses, avocado, cream cheese, low carb yogurt, avocado oil, coconut oil, and ghee. All meat is great to eat! Any type of berry is safe to consume in moderation. Sugar free candy, sugar free cake, sugar free cookies, and Keto friendly ice cream are ok to sample for sweet cravings occasionally. Use monkfruit for sweetener. Sugar free flavored syrups for coffee are safe. Drink sugar free beverages for flavored drink cravings. You can snack on pork skins (great replacement for bread crumbs to fry food in coconut or olive oil), Keto friendly chips, jerky, pickles, nuts, cheese, and sunflower seeds.

There are several cookie, pancake, waffle, and other sweet recipes that require almond or coconut flour, unsweetened cocoa powder, baking powder, and vanilla extract. Make sure you consume plenty of leafy greens and fiber filled vegetables daily to ensure that your diet is well balanced and healthiest for you. An increase in good cholesterol will likely happen on Keto. This is ok. However, improperly executed Keto can lead to high blood pressure or other diet correctable illnesses. Keto is not recommended for those diagnosed with Type I Diabetes.

Beware of the risk of Keto flu the first week or two. Dizziness, lightheadedness, tiredness, headaches, and or cramps while your body is changing it's fuel source from glucose and insulin to fat will occur. Imagine trying to change your vehicle's fueling source from gas to diesel... There will be some issues. Fortunately, our bodies will allow the luxury to change safely. Just stay mentally strong and patient while your body works it out! Salt, pickle juice, and sugar free sports drinks consumed to replace your electrolytes will minimize or prevent the Keto Flu.

Plateaus will happen after the 1-2 week "Keto Honeymoon" period. Do NOT be discouraged! After the initial 5lb. or more water weight loss; your body starts dealing with the real hard work of prepping to use fat as it's fueling source; and actually does it! This means a stall or plateau is inevitable. It could last a week or a few weeks. DO NOT BE DISCOURAGED OR STOP! Push through it to reach your fat flush. The fat flush process is as follows: Water weight falls off, fat cells begin to deflate, the fat sacks remain in your body waiting for you to relapse into your old way of eating for them to be refilled (DO NOT LET YOURSELF DOWN! You are doing this for your own personal improvement!), if you stay strong and starve those suckers out..... FAT FLUSH!!! It happens successfully when your body determines it's right for you. You will literally wake up a few pounds lighter one day. From that day forward, you will wake up almost everyday to some amount of weight loss. Other plateaus may occur naturally. In those instances; upgrading to strict Keto, any form of fasting, or a 3 day egg fast (a 3 day restrictive diet where all of your protein comes from eggs accompanied by cheese and healthy fats) may assist.

Comparison is the worst self inflicted obstacle. Please do not compare your progress to anyone else's! No one will have the same results because.... Well, you're you; and they are them. Now let's shop and uncook for Dirty Keto!

Shopping List: Make Your Own Combos for a Variety of Quick and Easy Keto Meals

- Green Salads
    - Spinach
    - 50/50 Blend
    - Kale Mix or any leafy green salad base you prefer
    - Tomatoes
    - Precooked Bacon
    - Strawberries
    - Blueberries
    - Raspberries
    - Blackberries
    - Cucumbers
    - Cheese
    - Avocados
    - Nuts
    - Parm Crisps (crushed for salad, whole for dipping)
    - Quest Chips (crushed for salad, whole for dipping)
    - Real Bacon Bits

- ◦ Boiled Eggs
- ◦ Tyson Cooked Fajita Chicken Strips
- ◦ Cooked Fajita Steak Strips
- ◦ Cooked Shrimp or any protein you'd like as a topping
- ◦ Kroger Brand or Newman's Seasoned Olive Oil and Vinegar Dressing (the best tasting dressing w/the least amount of carbs)
- Protein Based Salads (Stand Alone or as Sandwiches)
  - ◦ Tuna Salad (canned tuna)
  - ◦ Egg Salad (boiled eggs)
  - ◦ Chicken Salad (canned chicken)
  - ◦ Mayonnaise
  - ◦ Mustard
  - ◦ Celery Salt
  - ◦ Paprika
  - ◦ Salt
  - ◦ Black Pepper
  - ◦ Jalapeños
  - ◦ Peppers
  - ◦ Onion Powder
  - ◦ Garlic Powder
  - ◦ Dill Relish
  - ◦ Seasoned Salt
  - ◦ Vinegar
  - ◦ Spinach
  - ◦ Broccoli
  - ◦ Celery
  - ◦ Ranch Seasoning

- Sandwiches
- Hot Dogs
- Sausages
- Deli Meat or any protein you'd prefer
- Sola Bread
- La Banderita 5 Carb wraps (These can be cut, seasoned, and fried to be used for dipping like regular tortilla chips.)
- Birch Bender's Frozen Keto Waffles - **CHEAT CODE:** These are great for breakfast sandwiches w/ eggs, cheese, butter, sugar free syrup, and precooked bacon. Definitely easy, but you'll look like you are a true creative Chef, who put time and thought into this bacon, egg, and cheese McGriddle imposter!

I shall not expand any further here; as I just know even you Uncooks know how to make a sandwich to your liking! Just no PB&J, sugar cured meats, or Miracle Whip! The olive oil and vinegar salad dressing is delicious on sandwiches too.

***I typically use these products because they are the most reasonably priced and easiest to find locally for bread replacement (toast or heat them all before eating).**

- Scramblers: Yes, you need a skillet and heat. Don't worry, it takes 5 min. to throw together your easy, personalized, and delicious breakfast concoction.
  - Cooking Spray or Butter
  - Pre-diced Pico De Gallo
  - Eggs

- Spinach
- Mushrooms
- Cheese
- Real Bacon Bits
- Precooked Bacon

Don't be scared to get crazy and use any type of meat, pepper, or green veggies you'd prefer. You can season your meals w/any herbs and seasoning that you like; as long as it doesn't contain any sugar.

CHEAT CODE: Ore Ida's Just Crack an Egg Protein Cups are Microwaveable Deliciousness. I always season it and add 2 eggs and microwave it longer to cook completely.

***BONUS BREAKFAST IDEA: Breakfast Pizza. Throw parchment paper on a cookie sheet, spread shredded cheese for your "pizza crust," top it with your meat of choice, Italian seasoning, Veggies of choice, crack an egg over it, toss it in the oven for 10min., pull it out, and enjoy!**

- Snacks: Now these are life saving Keto Friendly goodness; and definitely major cheat codes! At times it'll act as your saving grace if you love sweets and adult beverages as much as I do!!! Please consume snacks sparingly and responsibly; as overconsumption can kick you out of Ketosis.
  - Rebel Ice Cream,
  - Enlightened Ice Cream
  - Swerve Cake Mix (Requires light cooking. Add Torani sugar free syrup for added flavor.)

- Swerve Cookie Mix (Requires light cooking. Add Torani sugar free syrup for added flavor.)
- Duncan Hines Walnut Brownie Cups (Add a splash of Torani's Sugar Free Salted Caramel Syrup to the mix too. Thank me later.)
- Quest Cookies (Microwave them for best taste. Can also be used for delicious ice cream sandwiches. Their bars are not Keto friendly for me.)
- Fat Snax Cookies
- High Key Snacks Cookies (This doubles as a great cereal substitute. Just dump a bag or 2 in your favorite bowl and pour on the unsweetened almond milk.)
- Carb Master Yogurt
- Sola Granola (Great cereal substitute, and with Carb Master Yogurt)
- Quest Chips (Sweet Chili is my favorite, but there are plenty of flavors.)
- Pork Skins (quickest nearly carb free way to meet your fat requirements for Macros)
- Sugar Free Hershey Plain or Caramel Bars
- Sugar Free Reese Cups
- Sugar Free Werther's Soft Caramel Chews
- Sugar Free Russell Stover's Candy
- Sugar Free Gummy Bears
- Sugar Free La Nouba Marshmallows

***Most of these items are typically found at and priced best at Walmart w/the exception of the Gummy Bears, which are**

mainly found at CVS; and the Quest Chips because the best flavors are found at GNC. Sugar free candy should be eaten sparingly; as it has a natural laxative effect when overly consumed, and you'll be glued to the nearest toilet if you can make it.

- Beverages
  - Coffee (Great with Torani Sugar Free Syrups and/or a splash of heavy cream)
  - Tea Bags (Great with lemon, monkfruit sweetener, or a splash of vanilla Torani Sugar Free Syrup)
  - Hot Chocolate (Mix Unsweetened Almond Milk, Unsweetened Cacao Powder, Sugar Free Torani Salted Caramel Syrup; and top it w/La Nouba Sugar Free Marshmallows, and melted Sugar Free Hershey Bars for your own Dirty Keto version of the hot chocolate featured on the cover.)
  - Unsweetened Almond Milk
  - Unsweetened Tea
  - Sparkling Ice
  - Gatorade Zero
  - Powerade Zero
  - Mio
  - Minute Maid Zero Sugar Mango Juice
  - Diet Coke
  - ALL OF THE WATER YOU CAN POSSIBLY CONSUME

CHEAT CODES FOR COCKTAIL IDEAS: Tequila w/ Coconut Pineapple or Lemon Lime Sparkling Ice, Unsweetened Lime Juice, or Minute Maid Zero Sugar Mango Juice and salt. Cognac w/Black Cherry Sparkling Ice or Diet Coke. Whiskey w/ Ginger Lime Sparkling Ice or Diet Coke and Splash of Unsweetened Lime Juice. Vodka and Coconut Pineapple Sparkling Ice, Minute Maid Zero Sugar any Flavor, or Mio and a Splash of Lime Juice. Corona Premier Beer, Pinot Grigio, Sauvignon Blanc, Merlot, and any Dry Unsweetened Wine is low carb enough to consume in moderation.

- Condiments Not Mentioned Above and Tips for Dining Out
  - G. Hughes has a line of sugar free condiments. (Get them all! They're delicious!)
  - Hot sauce,
  - Heinz Sugar Free Ketchup
  - Great Value Sugar Free Whipped Cream
  - Sugar Free Syrup

CHEAT CODE: Try your best to keep some of your substitutes for your triggers with you at all times! Survival Kit Example: Candy, packets of monkfruit sweetener (Splenda or your preferred sugar substitute is good), sugar free condiments (There are tiny containers you can put them in located in most stores' travel section), a 5 carb wrap or 2 slices of bread (This has saved me at the drive thru several times. Just order your sandwich w/o ketchup and bun w/a side salad.)

Dining Out

Remember you can eat out anywhere. Just order meat, green veggies or salad as sides, replace rice with riced cauliflower (you can also mash it for the mashed potato effect), diet or unsweetened beverages, or charcuterie, and you'll be just fine! Major Fast Food Cheat Codes are as follows:

- Hooter's and anywhere else that has naked wings w/hot or buffalo sauce are Keto Friendly
- Popeye's Chicken has blackened naked tenders
- Chick-fil-A has grilled nuggets
- Chipotle has Keto Bowls
- Five Guys has a burger bowl
- Jet's Pizza has cauliflower crust
- Olive Garden has zoodles (zucchini noodles)
- Jimmy John's also has an Unwich (lettuce wrap)
- Wendy's, Burger King, McDonalds, and any burger joint will accommodate serving your burger of choice w/o the bun and sugary ketchup
- Taco Bell has a Protein Plate

Quick Apps and Tools

- Download the Carb Manager App to help track everything you eat to make it easy to track your Macros. It does all of the math to calculate your calories and net carbs for you. It's also an awesome tool to scan items in the grocery store to ensure that they are suitable for your new Keto Lifestyle.
- Download the Zero App to keep you on track with intermittent fasting.
- Buy Ketone Test Strips from Amazon to be used daily in identifying whether or not you are in Ketosis; and helps to narrow down food items you may have consumed that knocked you out of Ketosis.

7

Conclusion

What's for you is for you on your personal Keto journey. People will question or judge what they don't understand. Understand that whatever you do to get the weight off for a healthier lifestyle is what you will have to do for the rest of your life. Otherwise, the weight comes back when you stop! If they ask you how long you're doing this; ask them how long they will eat the way they do! Just as they eat a "regular" diet and Vegetarians consume theirs; Keto is our way of life!

If you fall off of the Keto wagon; do NOT beat yourself up. Just use your progress and the reason you began this new way of life as renewed motivation to pick up where you left off! It's not a diet. It's a way of life!

***Please consult your Physician prior to starting this or any other major diet change. It is not recommended for those w/Diabetes Type I.**

Resources

I literally Googled Keto several times to retrieve information that was useful to me on my journey! No one site had enough factual information worth noting here. I also utilized Instagram to locate quite a bit of motivational material up to and including recipes and support groups throughout my journey. Lastly.... GOOD OLD COMMON SENSE! I just tried what sounded safest and best; and IT WORKED for me. Now, I'm filtering it all and making it plain for you! I wish you the best on your Keto Journey; and thank you so much for your support! Operation Get Finer starts NOW!!!